LEADERSHIP LESSONS IN QUOTES FOR ENTREPRENEURS & MANAGERS

BUSINESS WISDOM IN QUOTATIONS FOR QUICK TIPS, SPEECHES, PRESENTATIONS, MEETINGS, ARTICLES & ESSAYS

SANJAY GORA

The book is dedicated to

My lifelong learning partner and sounding board, my wife, Archana

&

My powerhouse of happiness, my daughter, Khushi

Contents

Space for Your favourite Quotes

Quotations in Alphabetical Order

·

A business that makes nothing but money is a poor business. (Henry Ford)

·

A businessman is a hybrid of a dancer and a calculator. (Paul Valery)

·

A champion is someone who gets up when he can't. (Jack Dempsey)

·

A diamond is merely a lump of coal that did well under pressure. (Henry Kissinger)

·

A fortress does not fall unless its towers are weakened. (SR Crawford)

·

A fresh start is not a new place, it is a mindset. (Rachel Wolchin)

·

A goal should scare you a little, and excite you a lot. (Joe Vitale)

·

A good compromise is one where everybody makes a contribution. (Angela Merkel)

·

A good example is the best sermon. (B Franklin)

•

A good leader is one that makes a positive impact and that impact should last a long time even in your absence. (Sheryl Sandberg)

•

A good story often increases the saleability of an item without increasing its actual value. (Roy H Williams)

•

A great future does not require a great post. (William Chapman)

•

A great man is hard on himself; a small man is hard on others. (Confucius)

•

A horse never runs so fast as when he has other horses to catch up and outpace. (Ovid)

•

A leader is best when people barely know that he exists, who talks little, when his work is done, his aim fulfilled, they will say, 'We did this ourselves.' (Lao Tzu)

•

A man never discloses his own character so clearly as when he describes another's. (JP Richter)

•

A man's worth is no greater than his ambitions.
(Marcus Aurelius)

•

A mind stretched by new experiences can never go back to its old dimensions. (Oliver Wendell Holmes Jr.)

•

A mistake repeated more than once is a decision.(Paulo Coelho)

•

A real decision is measured by the fact that you have taken a new action. If there is no action, you have not truly decided. (Tony Robbins)

•

A trusted advisor encourages you to look at a problem or opportunity from multiple angles. (Margo Georgiadis)

•

A year from now you may wish you had started today. (Karen Lamb)

•

Ability is what you're capable of doing. Motivation determines what you do. Attitude determines how well you do it. (Raymond Chandler)

•

Ability will never catch up with the demand for it. (Confucius)

•

Accept no one's definition of your life, define yourself. (Harvey Fierstein)

•

Act as if what you do makes a difference. It does. (William James)

•

Action is the most important key to any success. (Tony Robbins)

•

Activity itself is neither creative nor uncreative. You can paint in an uncreative way. You can sing in an uncreative way. You can clean the floor or cook in a creative way. Creativity is the quality that you bring to the activity you are doing. (Osho)

•

Adversity is the trial of principle. Without it, a man hardly knows whether he is honest or not. (Henry Fielding)

•

All birds find shelter during the rain. But, eagles avoid the rain by flying higher than the clouds. (Dr APJ Abdul Kalam)

•

All courses of action are risky, so prudence is not in avoiding danger (it's impossible), but calculating risk and acting decisively. Make mistakes of ambition and not mistakes of sloth. Develop the strength to do bold things, not the strength to suffer. (Niccolò Machiavelli)

•

All cruelty springs from weakness. (Seneca)

•

All diplomacy is a continuation of war by other means. (Zhou Enlai)

•

All generalizations are false, including this one. (Mark Twain)

•

All life is an experiment. The more experiments you make, the better. (Ralph Waldo Emerson)

•

All my life I wanted to be somebody. Now I see that I should have been more specific. (Jane Wagner)

•

Alone we can do so little; together we can do so much. (Helen Keller)

•

Always be a first-rate version of yourself, instead of a second-rate version of somebody else. (Judy Garland)

•

Always let losers have their words. (Francis Bacon)

•

Ambition is best not naked. (M Forbes)

·

An abnormal reaction to an abnormal situation is normal behavior. (Viktor Frankl)

·

An ant on the move does more than a dozing ox. (Lao Tzu)

·

An idea that is not dangerous is unworthy of being called an idea at all. (Oscar Wilde)

·

An idiot with a plan can beat a genius without a plan. (Warren Buffett)

·

And certainly we should take care not to make the intellect our god, it has, of course powerful muscles but no personality. It cannot lead, it can only serve, and it is not fastidious about its choice of leader. The intellect has a sharp eye for methods and tools, but it is blind to ends and values. (Einstein)

·

And if you think tough men are dangerous, wait until you see what weak men are capable of. (Jordan Peterson)

·

Apparently we have such an automatically positive reaction to compliments that we can fall victim to someone who uses them in an obvious attempt to win our favor. (Robert Cialdini)

•

Appear weak when you are strong, and strong when you are weak. (Sun Tzu)

•

Appreciation is a wonderful thing. It makes what is excellent in others belong to us as well. (Voltaire)

•

As long as you live, keep learning how to live. (Seneca)

•

As your faith is strengthened you will find that there is no longer the need to have a sense of control, and that things will flow as they will, and that you will flow with them, to your great delight and benefit. (Emmanuel Teney)

•

At first dreams seem impossible, then improbable, then inevitable. (Christopher Reeve)

•

In God we trust. All others must bring data. (W Edwards Deming)

•

A book is a dream that you hold in your hand. (Neil Gaiman)

•

Bad luck in small doses can cast a glittering light on the rest of life. (Ann Patchett)

•

Be humble. Be hungry. And always be the hardest worker in the room. (Dwayne Johnson)

•

Be kind, for everyone you meet is fighting a hard battle. (Plato)

•

Be patient and tough, someday this pain will be useful to you. (Ovid)

•

Be tolerant with others and strict with yourself. (Marcus Aurelius)

•

Be who you are and say what you feel because those who mind don't matter and those who matter don't mind. (Dr. Seuss)

•

Be who you are and the world will adjust. (VB Jones)

•

Behold the turtle. He only makes progress when he sticks his neck out. (James Bryant Conant)

•

Being yourself in a world that is constantly trying to make you something else is the greatest accomplishment. (RW Emerson)

•

Believe you can and you are halfway there.
(Theodore Roosevelt)

•

Benjamin Franklin may have discovered electricity
but it was the man who invented the meter who
made the money. (Earl Wilson)

•

Besides the noble art of getting things done, there is
the noble art of leaving things undone. The wisdom
of life consists in the elimination of non-essentials.
(Lin Yutang)

•

Better to do something imperfectly than to do
nothing perfectly. (Robert H Schuller)

•

Books are the bees which carry the quickening
pollen from one to another mind. (JR Lowell)

•

By failing to prepare, you are preparing to fail.
(Benjamin Franklin)

•

Care about what other people think and you will
always be their prisoner.(Lao Tzu)

•

Celebrate what you have accomplished, but also
raise the bar a little higher each time you succeed.
(Mia Hamm)

.

Champions keep playing until they get it right.
(Billie Jean King)

.

Change is hard at first, messy in the middle and
gorgeous at the end. (Robin Sharma)

.

Change is the law of life. And those who look only
to the past or present are certain to miss the future.
(John F Kennedy)

.

Character cannot be developed in ease and quiet.
Only through experience of trial and suffering can
the soul be strengthened, ambition inspired, and
success achieved. (Helen Keller)

.

Character is like pregnancy. It cannot be hidden
forever. (African proverb)

.

Character is much easier kept than recovered.
(Thomas Paine)

.

Character is what God and the angels know of us,
reputation is what men and women think of us.
(Horace Mann)

·

Character may almost be called the most effective
means of persuasion. (Aristotle)

·

Character may be manifested in the great moments,
but it is made in the small ones. (Winston
Churchill)

·

Circumstances don't make the man, they only reveal
him to himself. (Epictetus)

·

Communication is something so simple and difficult
that we can never put it in simple words. (TS
Matthews)

·

Competition brings out the best in products and the
worst in people. (David Sarnoff)

·

Competition is a rude yet effective motivation.
(Toba Beta)

·

Compromise makes a good umbrella but a poor roof
; it is a temporary expedient. (JR Lowell)

·

Concentrate all your thoughts upon the work at hand. The sun's rays do not burn until brought to a focus. (Alexander G Bell)

•

Consider not the present condition, but rather foresee the future and the end. A seed in the beginning is very small, but in the end a great tree. One should not consider the seed, but the tree and its abundance of blossoms, leaves and fruits. (Abdul Baha)

•

Content precedes design. Design in the absence of content is not design, it's decoration. (Jeffrey Zeldman)

•

Continuous improvement is better than delayed perfection. (Mark Twain)

•

Corporations have neither bodies to be kicked nor souls to be damned. (Andrew Jackson)

•

Corporations, which should be the carefully restrained creatures of the law and the servants of the people, are fast becoming the people's masters. (Grover Cleveland)

•

Courage does not always roar. Sometimes courage is the quiet voice at the end of the day, saying, "I will try again tomorrow."

•

Courage is tiny pieces of fear all glued together. (Terri Guillemets)

•

Courage stands halfway between cowardice and rashness, one of which is a lack, the other an excess of courage. (Plutarch)

•

Creativity is just connecting things. When you ask creative people how they did something, they feel a little guilty because they did not really do it, they just saw something. It seemed obvious to them after a while. (Steve Jobs)

•

Creativity is so delicate a flower that praise tends to make it bloom, while discouragement often nips it in the bud. Any of us will put out more and better ideas if our efforts are appreciated. (AF Osborn)

•

Criticism may not be agreeable, but it is necessary. It fulfils the same function as pain in the human body. It calls attention to an unhealthy state of things. (Winston Churchill)

•

Crocodiles are easy. They try to kill and eat you. People are harder. Sometimes they pretend to be your friend first. (Steve Irwin)

•

Design is not crafting a beautiful, textured button with breathtaking animation. It is figuring out if there is a way to get rid of the button altogether. (E Tufte)

•

Destroy negative thoughts when they first appear. This is when they are the weakest. (Songide Makwa)

•

Discipline is choosing between what you want now and what you want most. (Abraham Lincoln)

•

Discipline is the bridge between goals and accomplishment. (Jim Rohn)

•

Discussion is an exchange of knowledge, argument an exchange of ignorance. (Robert Quillen)

•

Do not free a camel of the burden of his hump; you may be freeing him from being a camel. (GK Chesterton)

•

Do not go where the path may lead ; go instead where there is no path and leave a trail. (RW Emerson)

•

Do not wait to strike till the iron is hot; make it hot by striking. (WB Yeats)

•

Do the best you can until you know better. Then when you know better, do better. (Maya Angelou)

•

Don't be pushed by your problems, be led by your dreams. (RW Emerson)

•

Don't count the days, make the days count. (M Ali)

•

Don't forget, while you are busy doubting yourself, someone else is admiring your strength. (Kristen Butter)

•

Don't let the concept of change scare you as much as the concept of staying unhappy. (Timber Hawkeye)

•

Don't mistake activity for achievement. (John Wooden)

•

Don't open a shop unless you know how to smile. (Jewish proverb)

•

Don't take criticism from people you would not take advice from. (Kyle Freedman)

•

Don't tell me what you value, show me your budget, and I will tell you what you value. (Joe Biden)

•

Don't wait. The time will never be just right. (Napoleon Hill)

•

Don't watch the clock, do what it does. Keep going. (Sam Levenson)

•

Don't be afraid to feel as angry or as loving as you can, because when you feel nothing, it's just death. (Lena Horne)

•

Efforts and courage are not enough without purpose and direction. (John F. Kennedy)

•

Ego says, once everything falls into place, I'll feel peace. Spirit says, Find your peace, and then everything will fall into place. (Marianne Williamson)

•

Enthusiasm is the master key to feeling great. It acts as a double energy boost. It keeps you positive and beyond the pull of negativity and also makes others feel good. Enthusiasm opens up a world of possibilities. (Dadi Janki)

•

Enthusiasm is the yeast that makes your hopes shine
to the stars. (Henry Ford)

•

Even a correct decision is wrong when it is taken
too late. (Lee Iacocca)

•

Even if you're on the right track, you'll get run over
if you just sit there. (Will Rogers)

•

Every great institution is the lengthened shadow of
a single man. (Thomas Edison)

•

Every single one of us has the potential to change
someone's life by just taking the time to listen to
them. (Steven Aitchison)

•

Everybody is a genius. But if you judge a fish by its
ability to climb a tree, it will live its whole life
believing that it is stupid. (Albert Einstein)

•

Everyone has somebody who can watch what you
are doing and give perspective. The one thing
people are never good at is seeing themselves as
others see them. A coach really, really helps.(Eric E.
Schmidt)

•

Everyone wants to live on top of the mountain, but all the happiness and growth occurs while you are climbing it. (Andy Rooney)

•

Everything can be taken from a man but one thing : the last of the human freedoms-to choose one's attitude in any given set of circumstances to choose one's own way. (Victor Frankl)

•

Everything you say should be true but not everything true should be said. (Voltaire)

•

Experience is not what happens to you, it's what you do with what happens to you. (Aldous Huxley)

•

Expertise is the enemy of innovation. (Stephen Shapiro)

•

Faced with the choice between changing one's mind and proving that there is no need to do so, almost everyone gets busy on the proof. (JK Galbraith)

•

Facts are stubborn things, but statistics are pliable. (Mark Twain)

•

Facts do not cease to exist because they are ignored. (AL Huxley)

•

Failure is a feeling long before it is an actual result. (Michelle Obama)

•

Failure is a trickster with a keen sense of irony and cunning. It takes great delight in tripping one when success is almost within reach. (N Hill)

•

Failure is an option here. If things are not failing, you are not innovating enough. (Elon Musk)

•

Failure is the condiment that gives success its flavor. (Truman Capote)

•

Failure should be our teacher, not our undertaker. Failure is delay, not defeat. It is a temporary detour, not a dead end. Failure is something we can avoid only by saying nothing, doing nothing, and being nothing. (Denis Waitley)

•

Faith is taking the first step even when you don't see the whole staircase. (Martin Luther King, Jr)

•

Faith makes many of the mountains which it has to remove. (Dean WR Inge)

.

Fear can keep us up all night long, but faith makes one fine pillow. (Philip Gulley)

.

Few will have the greatness to bend history itself, but each of us can work to change a small portion of events, and in the total of all those acts will be written the history of this generation. (Bobby Kennedy)

.

Finish each day and be done with it. You have done what you could. Some blunders and absurdities no doubt crept in, forget them as soon as you can. Tomorrow is a new day. (RW Emerson)

.

First, see clearly. Next, act correctly. Finally, endure and accept the world as it is. (Ryan Holiday)

.

Follow your heart but take your brain with you. (Alfred Adler)

.

For myself I am an optimist – it does not seem to be much use to be anything else. (Winston S. Churchill)

.

For what it is worth : it is never too late to be whoever you want to be. I hope you live a life you are proud of, and if you find that you are not, I hope you have the strength to start over. (F. Scott

Fitzgerald)

•

For you to insult me, I must first value your opinion.
(Joubert Botha)

•

Fuel is not sold in a forest, nor fish on a lake.
(Chinese proverb)

•

Good communication is as stimulating as black
coffee, and just as hard to sleep after. (Anne M
Lindbergh)

•

Gratitude makes sense of the past, brings peace for
today, and creates a vision for tomorrow. (Melody
Beattie)

•

Gratitude unlocks the fullness of life. It turns what
we have into enough. (Melody Beattie)

•

Great spirits have often encountered violent
opposition from weak minds. (Albert Einstein)

•

Growth for the sake of growth is the ideology of the
cancer cell. (Edward Abbey)

•

Hard work will always overcome natural talent
when natural talent does not work hard enough.

(Sir Alex Ferguson)

•

Having a dream you don't pursue is like buying an ice-cream cone and watching it melt all over your hand. (Frank Papasso)

•

He that would govern others first should be the master of himself. (Philip M)

•

He was a self-made man who owed his lack of success to nobody. (Joseph Heller)

•

He who asks a question is fool for a minute, the man who does not is a fool for life. (Chinese Proverb)

•

He who does not desire power is fit to hold it. (Plato)

•

He who does not offend cannot be honest. (Thomas Paine)

•

He who hesitates gets bumped from the rear. (Homer Phillips)

•

He, who has a why to live for, can bear almost any how. (Friedrich Nietzsche)

•

Here is a test to find out whether your mission in life is complete. If you are alive, it is not.(Lauren Bacall)

•

Heroism does not always happen in a burst of glory. Sometimes small triumphs and large hearts change the course of history. (Mary Roach)

•

Hire people who are better than you are, then leave them to get on with it. (David Ogilvy)

•

Hold fast to dreams, for if dreams die, life is a broken winged bird that cannot fly. (Langston Hughes)

•

Hope is like a road in the country; there was never a road, but when many people walk on it, the road comes into existence. (Lyn Yutang)

•

Hope is the thing with feathers that perches in the soul- and sings the tunes without the words- and never stops at all. (Emily Dickinson)

•

How long are you going to wait before you demand the best for yourself? (Epictetus)

•

Human communication permeates the human condition. Human communication surrounds us and is an in-built aspect of everything human beings are and do. That makes any effort to explain, predict, to some extent control human communication a pretty big order. How does one get a handle on the totality of human communication? (Frank Dance)

·

Humility is about refusing to get all tangled up with yourself. It is about surrender, receptivity, awareness, simplicity. Breathing in. Breathing out. (Cheryl Strayed)

·

Humility is not renunciation of pride but the substitution of one pride for another. (Eric Hoffer)

·

Humility is not thinking less of yourself ; it is thinking of yourself less. (Rick Warren)

·

Humility is the core virtue which is instrumental in allowing our other virtues to shine.(Xenophon)

·

Humility makes great men twice honorable. (Benjamin Franklin)

·

I am careful not to confuse excellence with perfection. Excellence I can reach for, perfection is God's business. (Michael Fox)

•

I am not a product of my circumstances. I am a product of my decisions. (Stephen R Covey)

•

I am not what happened to me, I am what I choose to become. (CG Jung)

•

I can't tell you the key to success, but the key to failure is trying to please everyone. (Ed Sheeran)

•

I can't understand why people are frightened of new ideas. I am frightened of the old ones. (John Cage)

•

I cannot remember the books I've read any more than the meals I have eaten; even so, they have made me. (Ralph Waldo Emerson)

•

I can't understand why people are frightened of new ideas. I'm frightened of the old ones. (John Cage)

•

I could not find the sports car of my dreams, so I built it myself. (F Porsche)

•

I did not get there by wishing for it or hoping for it, but by working for it. (Estee Lauder)

•

I fear not the man who has practiced 10,000 kicks once, but I fear the man who had practiced one kick 10,000 times. (Bruce Lee)

•

I have an absolute rule. I refuse to make a decision that somebody else can make. The first rule of leadership is to save yourself for the big decision. Don't allow your mind to become cluttered with the trivia. Don't let yourself become the issue. (Richard Nixon)

•

I have been impressed with the urgency of doing. Knowing is not enough, we must apply. Being willing is not enough, we must do. (Leonardo Da Vinci)

•

I have failed many times, but I have never gone into a game expecting myself to fail. (Michael Jordan)

•

I have learnt over the years that when one's mind is made up, this diminishes fear, knowing what must be done does away with fear. (Rosa Parks)

•

I have never seen any life transformation that did not begin with the person finally getting tired of their own bullshit. (Elizabeth Gilbert)

•

I never wanted to be the next Bruce Lee. I just wanted to be the first Jackie Chan. (Jackie Chan)

•

I sometimes feel I have nothing to say, and I want to communicate this. (Damien Hirst)

•

I think failure is nothing more than life's way of nudging you that you are off course. (Sara Blakely)

•

I will give you a definite maybe. (Samuel Goldwyn)

•

I will go anywhere as long as it is forward. (David Livingston)

•

I would rather be vaguely right than precisely wrong. (JM Keynes)

•

If A is success in life, then A=x+y+z. Work is x, play is y, and z is keeping your mouth shut. (Albert Einstein)

•

If I had an hour to solve a problem, I would spend fifty-five minutes thinking about the problem. (Albert Einstein)

•

If I had asked people what they wanted, they would have said faster horses. (Henry Ford)

•

If I have a thousand ideas and only one turns out to be good, I am satisfied. (Alfred Nobel)

•

If i waited until I had all my ducks in a row, I'd never get across the street. Sometimes you just have to gather up what you have got and make a run for it. (Judge Lynn Toler)

•

If it was not hard, everyone would do it. The hard is what makes it great. (Tom Hanks)

•

If most of us remain ignorant of ourselves, it is because self-knowledge is painful and we prefer the pleasures of illusion. (Aldous Huxley)

•

If people are not laughing at your goals, your goals are too small. (Azim Premji)

•

If people like you, they will listen to you. But if they trust you, they will do business with you. (Zig Ziglar)

•

If things go wrong, don't go with them. (Roger Babson)

•

If we command our wealth, we shall be rich and free, if our wealth commands us, we are poor indeed. (Edmund Burke)

•

If you anticipate the coming of troubles, you take away their power when they arrive. (Seneca)

•

If you are not going all the way, why go at all? (Joe Namath)

•

If you are not willing to risk the usual, you will have to settle for the ordinary. (Jim Rohn)

•

If you bet on a horse, that is gambling. If you bet you can make three spades, that is entertainment. If you bet cotton will go up three points, that is business. See the difference? (Blackie Sherrode)

•

If you can change your mind, you can change your life. (William James)

•

If you can't fly then run. If you can't run then walk, if you can't walk then crawl. But whatever you do you have to keep moving forward. (Martin Luther King Jr.)

•

If you can't outplay them. Outwork them. (Ben Hogan)

•

If you celebrate your differentness, the world will, too. It believes exactly what you tell it—through the words you use to describe yourself, the actions you take to care for yourself, and the choices you make to express yourself. (Victoria Moran)

•

If you cry because the sun has gone out of your life, your tears will prevent you from seeing the stars. (R Tagore)

•

If you don't have time for things that matter, stop doing things that don't. (Courtney Carver)

•

If you don't know where you are going, any road will get you there. (Lewis Carroll)

•

If you give me six hours to chop down a tree, I will spend the first four hours sharpening my axe. (Abraham Lincoln)

•

If you hang out with chickens, you are going to cluck and if you hangout with eagles, you are going to fly. (Dr. Steve Maraboli)

•

If you know what somebody wants, you know what he is like. (WH Auden)

•

If you think adventure is dangerous, try normal; it's lethal. (Paulo Coelho)

•

If you think you can do a thing or think you can't do a thing, you are right. (Henry Ford)

•

If you view things that happen to you, both good and bad, as opportunities, then you operate out of a higher level of consciousness. (Les Brown)

•

If you want something new, you have to stop doing something old. (Peter Drucker)

•

If you want to be happy, set a goal that commands your thoughts, liberates your energy & inspires your hopes. (A. Carnegie)

•

If you want to change attitudes, start with a change in behaviours. (Katharine Hepburn)

•

If you want to have enough to give to others, you will need to take care of yourself first. A tree that refuses water and sunlight for itself can't bear fruits for others. (Emily Maroutian)

•

If you want to master a habit, the key is to start with repetition, not perfection..(James Clear)

•

If you wish to improve, be content to appear clueless or stupid. (Epictetus)

•

If your compassion does not include yourself, it is incomplete. (Buddha)

•

In a conflict between the heart and the brain, follow your heart. (Swami Vivekananda)

•

In a wide variety of human activity, achievement is not possible without discomfort. (Alex Hutchinson)

•

In business, when two people always agree, one of them is irrelevant. (William Wrigley)

•

In each human heart are a tiger, a pig, an ass and a nightingale. Diversity of character is due to their unequal activity. (A Bierce)

•

In every work of genius we recognize our own rejected thoughts, they come back to us with a certain alienated majesty. (RW Emerson)

•

In order to be irreplaceable one must always be different. (Coco Chanel)

•

In the business world, everyone is paid in two coins : cash and experience. Take the experience first ; the cash will come later. (Harold Geneen)

•

In the depth of winter, I finally learned that within me there lay an invincible summer. (Albert Camus)

•

In the end, all business operations can be reduced to three words : people, product and profits. Unless you have got a good team, you can't do much with the other two. (Lee Iacocca)

•

In the end, it is impossible not to become what others believe you are. (Caesar)

•

In the end, we only regret the chances we didn't take. (Lewis Carroll)

•

In the information society, nobody thinks. We expected to banish paper, but we actually banished thought. (Michael Crichton)

•

In the midst of change we often discover wings we never knew we had. (Ekaterina Walter)

In three words I can sum up everything I have learned about life : it goes on. (Robert Frost)

Influence is the new power. If you have influence, you can create a brand. (Michelle Phan)

Inspirations never go in for long engagements, they demand immediate marriage to action. (B Francis)

Instead of worrying about what you cannot control, shift your energy to what you can create. (Roy T. Bennett)

Integrity is telling myself the truth. And honesty is telling the truth to other people. (Spencer Johnson)

Intellect distinguishes between the possible and the impossible ; reason distinguishes between the sensible and the senseless. Even the possible can be senseless. (Max Born)

Intelligence is not to make no mistakes, but quickly to see how to make them good. (Bertolt Brecht)

Intelligence without ambition is a bird without wings. (Salvador Dali)

•

Invention, it must be humbly admitted, does not consist in creating out of void but out of chaos. (Mary Shelley)

•

Investing in a startup does not make you an entrepreneur any more than buying a grand piano makes you a concert pianist. (Jeffrey Fry)

•

Investing should be more like watching paint dry or watching grass grow. If you want excitement, take $800 and go to Las Vegas. (Paul Samuelson)

•

It does not matter how slowly you go as long as you do not stop. (Confucius)

•

It is a blessed thing that in every age someone has had the individuality enough and courage enough to stand by his own convictions. (Robert G. Ingersoll)

•

It is a fundamental law of nature that in order to gain strength one has to push one's limits, which is painful. (Ray Dalio)

•

It is a paradoxical but profoundly true and important principle of life that the most likely way to reach a goal is to be aiming not at that goal itself but at some more ambitious goal beyond it. (Arnold Joseph Toynbee)

•

It is better and more praiseworthy to be well-read in the book of experience, the teacher of the teachers. (Leonardo de Vinci)

•

It is curious that physical courage should be so common in the world and moral courage so rare. (Mark Twain)

•

It is hard to imagine a more stupid or more dangerous way of making decisions than by putting those decisions in the hands of people who pay no price for being wrong. (Thomas Sewell)

•

It is important to remember that there are no overnight successes. You will need to be dedicated, single-minded and there is no substitute for hard work. (Mukesh Ambani)

•

It is impossible for someone to learn what they think they already know. (Epictetus)

•

It is never too late to be what you might have been.
(George Eliot)

•

It is not because things are difficult that we do not
dare, it is because we do not dare that they are
difficult. (Seneca)

•

It is not from the benevolence of the butcher, the
brewer, or the baker that we expect our dinner, but
from their regard to their own interest. (Adam
Smith)

•

It is ok if you fall down and lose your spark. Just
make sure that when you get back up, you rise as
the whole damn fire. (Colette Werden)

•

It is our choices that show what we truly are, far
more than our abilities. (J.K. Rowling)

•

It isn't where you came from; it's where you're
going that counts. (Ella Fitzgerald)

•

It takes a lot of courage to show your dreams to
someone else. (Erma Bombeck)

•

It takes less time to do a thing right than to explain
why you did it wrong. (Longfellow)

•

It's not business to consumer, it is not business to business, it is people to people. (Brian Solis)

•

Kites rise highest against the wind, not with it. (Winston S. Churchill)

•

Leadership is the self-confidence of working with people smarter than you.(Azim Premji)

•

Let a man lose everything else in the world but his enthusiasm and he will come through again. (H. W. Arnold)

•

Let gratitude be the pillow upon which you kneel to say your nightly prayer. (Maya Angelou)

•

Life became a lot simpler when I decided just to let some people misunderstand me. (Alicia Lockhard)

•

Life can only be understood backwards, but it must be lived forwards. (Soren Kierkegaard)

•

Love the hand that fate deals you and play it as your own. (Marcus Aurelius)

•

Luck is what happens when preparation meets opportunity. (Seneca)

•

Magic happens when you don't give up, even though you want to. The universe always falls in love with a stubborn heart. (JM Storm)

•

Make blessing others part of your work day. (Mary Davis)

•

Make failure your teacher, not your undertaker. (Zig Ziglar)

•

Make yourself a priority once in a while. It's not selfish. It's necessary. (Karen A. Baquiran)

•

May we stop seeing ourselves through the eyes of people who never saw us. (Shane Steele)

•

May your choices reflect your hopes, not your fears. (Nelson Mandela)

•

Men of genius are often dull and inert in society ; as the blazing meteor, when it descends to earth, is only a stone. (Henry Longfellow)

•

My attitude was that competition could try to copy
my style but they can't read my mind so I will leave
them a mile and a half behind. (Ray Kroc)

•

Never argue with stupid people, because they will
drag you down to their level and then beat you with
experience.(Mark Twain)

•

Never assume that loud is strong and quiet is weak.
(Anon)

•

Never attack the Performer, attack his Performance.
(Lou Holtz)

•

Never compete with someone who has nothing to
lose. (B Gracian)

•

Never give up, for that is just the place and time
that the tide will turn. (Harriet Beecher Stowe)

•

Never make a permanent decision based on a
temporary storm. No matter how raging the billows
are today, remind yourself : This too shall pass. (TD
Jakes)

•

New beginnings are often disguised as painful
endings. (Lao Tzu)

•

No army can withstand the strength of an idea
whose time has come. (Victor Hugo)

•

No experiment is ever a complete failure. It can
always be used as a bad example. (P.Dickson)

•

No great genius has ever existed without some
touch of madness. (Aristotle)

•

No one changes the world who is not obsessed.
(Billie Jean King)

•

No one has ever made himself great by showing how
small someone else is. (Irvin Himmel)

•

Nobody who ever gave their best regretted it.
(George Halas)

•

Normal is not something to aspire for, it is
something to get away from. (Jodie Foster)

•

Not what we say about our blessings, but how we
use them, is the true measure of our thanksgiving.
(Purkiser)

•

Nothing has any power over me other than that which I give it through my conscious thoughts. (Tony Robbins)

•

Nothing is more difficult, and therefore more precious, than to be able to decide. (Napoleon Bonaparte)

•

Now, more than ever, business leaders need to invest time and energy into improving their networks. (Dan Schawbel)

•

Obsessions are the only things that matter. (Patricia Highsmith)

•

Obstacles are those frightful things you see when you take your eyes off the goal. (Henry Ford)

•

One discovers the light in darkness, that is what darkness is for ; but everything in our lives depends on how we bear the light. (James Baldwin)

•

One of the funny things about the stock market is that every time one person buys, another sells, and both think they are astute. (W Feather)

•

One reason so few of us achieve what we truly want is that we never direct our focus, we never concentrate our power. Most people dabble their way through life, never deciding to master anything in particular. (Tony Robbins)

•

Only those who dare to fail greatly can ever achieve greatly. (RF Kennedy)

•

Only those who will risk going too far can possibly find out how far one can go. (TS Eliot)

•

Our fingerprints don't fade from the lives we have touched.(Will Fetters)

•

Patience and persistence are the providers of progress. (Tim Fargo)

•

Pause before judging. Pause before assuming. Pause before accusing. Pause whenever you are about to react harshly and you will avoid doing and saying things you will later regret. (Lori Deschene)

•

People do not decide their futures, they decide their habits and their habits decide their futures. (FM Alexander)

•

People do not seem to realise that their opinion of the world is also a confession of character. (RW Emerson)

•

People forget how fast you did a job, but they remember how well you did it. (Howard W. Newton)

•

People may hear your words, but they feel your attitude. (John C Maxwell)

•

People will do things in a boardroom that they would never do as an individual. Group decisions, no personal liability. (Richard Schaden)

•

Purpose-driven leaders tap into the deep well of intrinsic motivation inside themselves and those around them. (Aaron Hurst)

•

Raise your words, not your voice. It is rain that grows flowers, not thunder. (Rumi)

•

Reach for the stars, even if you have to stand on a cactus. (Susan Longacre)

•

Read the best books first, or you may not have a chance to read them at all. (HD Thoreau)

•

Readers are of two sorts, one who carefully goes through a book, and the other who as carefully lets the book go through him. (Douglas Jerrold)

•

Real difficulties can be overcome, it is only the imaginary ones that are unconquerable. (TN Vail)

•

Reject your sense of injury and the injury itself disappears. (Marcus Aurelius)

•

Reputation is a bubble which bursts when a man tries to blow it up for himself. (Emma Carleton)

•

Rest is not idle, is not wasteful. Sometimes rest is the most productive thing you can do for body and soul. (Erica Layne)

•

Rich colours actually look more luminous on a grey day, because they are seen against a somber background and seem to be burning with a lustre of their own. Against a dark sky all flowers look like fireworks. (GK Chesterton)

•

Science may never come up with a better office communication system than the coffee break. (Earl Wilson)

•

Scratch the surface in a typical boardroom and we are all just cavemen with briefcases, hungry for a wise person to tell our stories. (Alan Kay)

•

Set your mind on a definite goal and observe how quickly the world stands aside to let you pass. (Napoleon Hill)

•

Some people are going to reject you simply because you shine too bright for them. That is okay. Keep shining. (Mandy Hale)

•

Some people dream of success, while other people get up every morning and make it happen. (Wayne Huizenga)

•

Some people will never like you because your spirit irritates their demons. (Denzel Washington)

•

Some persons are very decisive when it comes to avoiding decisions. (Brendan Francis)

•

Somebody once said that in looking for people to hire, you look for three qualities- integrity, intelligence and energy. And if they don't have the first, the other two will kill you. You think about it, it's true. If you hire somebody without the first, you really want them dumb and lazy. (Warren Buffet)

•

Sometimes not getting what you want is a wonderful stroke of luck. (Dalai Lama)

•

Sometimes you second guess yourself because you were taught that it was your job to be responsible for how others would react to your choices. (Yasmine Cheyenne)

•

Sometimes your only available transportation is a leap of faith. (Margaret Shepherd)

•

Somewhere in the world there is a defeat for everyone. Some are destroyed by defeat, and some made small and mean by victory. Greatness lives in one who triumphs equally over defeat and victory. (John Steinbeck)

•

Stay committed to your decisions, but stay flexible in your approach. (Tony Robbins)

•

Stay strong, make them wonder how you are still smiling. (Anon)

•

Stop acting so small. You are the universe in ecstatic motion. (Rumi)

•

Stop being afraid of what could go wrong, and start being excited for what could go right. (Tony Robbins)

•

Strong people don't put others down. They lift them up. (Darth Vader)

•

Success is a journey, not a destination. The doing is often more important than the outcome. (Arthur Ashe)

•

Success usually comes to those who are too busy to be looking for it. (Henry David Thoreau)

•

Successful people have libraries. The rest have big screen TVs. (Jim Rohn)

•

Take chances, make mistakes. That is how you grow. Pain nourishes your courage. You have to fail in order to practice being brave. (Mary Tyler Moore)

•

Take integrity over popularity and you will always be cool. (Carlos Santana)

•

Take up one idea. Make that one idea your life- think of it, dream of it, live on that idea. Let the brain, muscles, nerves, every part of your body be full of that idea, and just leave every other idea alone. This is the way to success. (Swami Vivekananda)

•

Taking initiative pays off. It is hard to visualise someone as a leader if she is always waiting to be told what to do. (Sheryl Sandberg)

•

Talent hits a target no one else can hit ; Genius hits a target no one else can see. (Arthur Schopenhauer)

•

Tales of failure, awkwardness, misfortune, danger , or disaster, told authentically, hastens deep engagement. (Chris Anderson)

•

That men do not learn very much from the lessons of history is the most important of all the lessons that history has to teach. (Aldous Huxley)

•

The aim of argument should not be victory, but progress. (Karl Popper)

•

The aim of argument, or of discussion, should not be victory, but progress. (Joseph Joubert)

•

The Art of communication is the language of leadership. (James Humes)

•

The art of progress is to preserve order amid change and to preserve change amid order. (AN Whitehead)

•

The best gift you are ever going to give someone- the permission to feel safe in their own skin to feel worthy. To feel like they are enough. (Hannah Brencher)

•

The best is the enemy of the good. (Voltaire)

•

The best revenge is not to be like your enemy. (Marcus Aurelius)

•

The cave you fear to enter may hold the light you seek. (Rumi)

•

The chains of habit are too weak to be felt until they are too strong to be broken. (Samuel Johnson)

•

The creation of a thousand forests is in one acorn. (RW Emerson)

•

The Creator has not given you a longing to do that which you have no ability to do. (OS Marden)

•

The difference between ordinary and extraordinary is that little extra. (Jimmy Johnson)

•

The displacement of a little sand can change occasionally the course of a deep river. (MG Prada)

•

The fears we don't face become our limits. (Zig Ziglar)

•

The fire in you was never meant to be tamed. Those flames are meant to light the world. (Barbara Gianquitto)

•

The first step to getting the things you want out of life is this. Decide what you want. (Ben Stein)

•

The future belongs to those who believe in the beauty of their dreams. (Eleanor Roosevelt)

•

The greatest discovery of my generation is that human beings can alter their lives by altering their attitudes of mind. (W James)

•

The greatest enemy of knowledge is not ignorance, it is the illusion of knowledge. (Stephen Hawking)

•

The greatest use of life is to spend it on something that will outlast it. (Willaim James)

•

The harder I work, the luckier I get. (Gary Player)

•

The highest use of capital is not to make more money, but to make money to do more for the betterment of life. (Henry Ford)

•

The intellect is blind and cannot move of itself-it is an inactive, secondary help, the real help is feeling, love. Intellect is like limbs without the power of locomotion. It is only when feeling enters and gives them motion that they move and work on others. It is the heart that takes one to the highest place, which intellect can never reach. It goes beyond intellect and reaches what is called inspiration. (Swami Vivekananda)

•

The joy we feel has little to do with the circumstances of our lives and everything to do with the focus of our lives. (RM Nelson)

•

The man we call a specialist today was formerly called a man with a one-track mind. (Endre Balogh)

•

The man who goes alone can start today; but he who travels with another must wait till that other is ready. (Henry David Thoreau)

•

The megalomaniac differs from the narcissist by the fact that he wishes to be powerful rather than charming, and seeks to be feared rather than loved. To this type belong many lunatics and most of the great men of history. (B Russell)

•

The merit of a man is not in the knowledge he possesses, but in the effort he made to achieve it. (GE Lessing)

•

The more violent the storm, the quicker it passes. (Paulo Coelho)

•

The most basic question is not what is best, but who shall decide what is best. (Thomas Sowell)

•

The most courageous act is still to think for yourself. Aloud. (Coco Chanel)

•

The most difficult thing is the decision to act, the rest is merely tenacity. The fears are paper tigers. You can do anything you decide to do. You can act to change and control your life, and the procedure, the process is its own reward. (Amelia Earhart)

•

The most effective way to do it is to do it. (Amelia Earhart)

•

The move you are scared to make might be the game changer. (Anon)

•

The only measure of success is joy. (Deepak Chopra)

•

The only problem we really have is we think we are not supposed to have problems! Problems call us to higher level- face & solve them now. (Tony Robbins)

•

The only real limitation is the one you accept & set up in your own mind. (Napoleon Hill)

•

The only tyrant I accept in this world is the 'still small voice' within me. And even though I have to face the prospect of being a minority of one, I humbly believe I have the courage to be in such a hopeless minority. (Mahatma Gandhi)

•

The opposite of courage in our society isn't cowardice, it's conformity. (Rollo May)

•

The pessimist sees difficulty in every opportunity. The optimist sees opportunity in every difficult situation. (Winston Churchill)

·

The price of anything is the amount of life you exchange for it. (HD Thoreau)

·

The reading of all good books is like a conversation with the finest men of past centuries. (Rene Descartes)

·

The secret of change is to focus all of your energy, not on fighting the old, but on building the new. (Dan Millman)

·

The secret of genius is to carry the spirit of the child into old age, which means never losing your enthusiasm. (Aldous Huxley)

·

The secret of getting ahead is getting started. The secret of getting started is breaking your complex overwhelming tasks into small manageable tasks, and starting on the first one. (Mark Twain)

·

The secret of my influence has always been that it remained secret. (Salvador Dali)

·

The secret of success of every man and woman who has ever been successful lies in the fact that they formed the habit of doing things that failures don't like to do. (Albert EN Gray)

•

The secret to change is to focus all of your energy, not on fighting the old, but on building the new. (Socrates)

•

The single biggest problem in communication is the illusion that it has taken place. (GB Shaw)

•

The smallest deed is better than the greatest intention. (John Burroughs)

•

The smallest seed of faith is better than the largest fruit of happiness. (HD Thoreau)

•

The Stock market is a device to transfer money from the impatient to the patient. (Warren Buffett)

•

The successful warrior is the average man, with laser-like focus. (Bruce Lee)

•

The test of first-rate intelligence is the ability to hold two opposed ideas in mind at the same time and still retain the ability to function. (F Scott Fitzgerald)

•

The time your game is most vulnerable is when you are ahead. Never let up. (Rod Laver)

·

The trouble with most of us is that we would rather be ruined by praise than saved by criticism. (Norman Vincent Peale)

·

The very least you can do in your life is to figure out what you hope for. And the most you can do is live inside that hope. (Barbara Kingsolver)

·

The voice of the intelligence is drowned out by the roar of fear. It is ignored by the voice of desire. It is contradicted by the voice of shame. It is biased by hate and extinguished by anger. Most of all it is silenced by ignorance. (Karl A. Menninger)

·

The way I see it, if you want the rainbow, you gotta put up with the rain. (Dolly Parton)

·

The way to find a needle in a haystack is to sit down. (Beryl Markham)

·

The winds and waves are always on the side of the ablest navigators. (Edward Gibbon)

·

The world is an oyster but you don't crack it open on a mattress. (Arthur Miller)

•

The world is changed by your example not by your opinion. (Paulo Coelho)

•

The world is more malleable than you think, and it's waiting for you to hammer it into shape. (Bono)

•

There are a great many opinions in this world, and a good half of them are professed by people who have never been in trouble. (Anton Chekhov)

•

There are many ways of going forward, but only one way of standing still. (Franklin Delano Roosevelt)

•

There are no traffic jams along the extra mile. (Roger Staubach)

•

There are two ways of spreading light : to be the candle or the mirror that reflects it. (Edith Wharton)

•

There can be powerful, hard-earned incentives to hold back certain truths. (Frei & Morris)

•

There is a phrase in Buddhism , 'Beginner's mind'. It is wonderful to have a beginner's mind. (Steve Jobs)

•

There is always more waiting for you on the other side of fear. (Elaine Welteroth)

•

There is no medicine like hope, no incentive so great, and no tonic so powerful as expectation of something tomorrow. (OS Marden)

•

There is no other way to guard yourself against flattery than by making men understand that telling you the truth will not offend you. (Niccolò Machiavelli)

•

There is no shame in admitting that you were previously speaking from a less informed place. (Kelly Hayes)

•

There is no such thing as work-life balance. There are work-life choices, and you make them, and they have consequences. (Jack Welch)

•

There is no way to make people like change. You can only make them feel less threatened by it. (FO Hayes)

•

There is nothing more deceptive than an obvious fact. (Arthur C Doyle)

•

There is one thing stronger than all the armies in the world : and that is an idea whose time has come. (Victor Hugo)

•

There is only one way to avoid criticism : do nothing, say nothing , and be nothing. (Aristotle)

•

There is something magical about beginnings, about the challenges that come with territory not yet conquered, about being the underdog. I think I would far rather stand at the beginning of something, looking up, rather than at a summit, looking down. (Jo Malone)

•

There is something that is much more scarce, something rarer than ability. It is the ability to recognize ability. (Robert Half)

•

There is the happiness which comes from creative effort. The joy of dreaming, creating, building, whether in painting a picture, writing an epic, singing a song, composing a symphony, devising new invention, creating a vast industry. (Henry Miller)

•

There is zero correlation between being the best talker and having the best ideas. (Susan Cain)

.

Things which matter most must never be at the mercy of things which matter least. (Goethe)

.

Those not chasing their dreams should stay out of the way of those who are. (Tim Fargo)

.

Those who do not move, do not notice their chains. (Rosa Luxemburg)

.

Though nobody can go back and make a new beginning... Anyone can start over and make a new ending. (Chico Xavier)

.

Through imagination, we can visualise the uncreated worlds of potential that lie within us. (Stephen R Covey)

.

To be great, truly great, you have to be the kind of person who makes the others around you great. (Mark Twain)

.

To be irreplaceable, one must always be different. (Coco Chanel)

.

To be nobody but yourself in a world which is doing its best, night and day, to make you everybody else means to fight the hardest battle which any human being can fight, and never stop fighting. (EE Cummings)

•

To change fate, you do not choose small steps. (Amy Tan)

•

To dare is to lose one's footing momentarily. Not to dare is to lose oneself. (Soren Kierkegaard)

•

To know ten thousand things, know one well. (Miyamoto Musashi)

•

To make a difference in someone's life, you don't have to be brilliant, rich, beautiful or perfect. You just have to care. (Mandy Hale)

•

To read without reflecting is like eating without digesting. (Edmund Burke)

•

Tomorrow belongs to the people who prepare for it today. (Malcolm X)

•

Too many of us are not living our dreams because we are living our fears. (Les Brown)

•

Treat others as if they already are the shining light they are capable of becoming. (Mary Davis)

•

True courage is not the brutal force of vulgar heroes, but the firm resolve of virtue and reason. (AN Whitehead)

•

Trust is like the air we breathe- when it is present, nobody really notices ; when it is absent, everybody notices. (Warren Buffett)

•

Trust yourself. You know more than you think you do. (Benjamin Spock)

•

Unexpected kindness is the most powerful, least costly, and most underrated agent of human change. (Bob Kerrey)

•

Upheavals sieve the big men from the little. (BC Forbes)

•

Usually when people are sad, they don't do anything. They just cry over their condition. But when they get angry, they bring about a change. (Malcolm X)

•

Value judgements are not to be established on the basis of facts- and that is a fact. (JW Krutch)

•

Value those people who tell you the truth, not just those people who tell you what you want to hear. (Pat Summitt)

•

We all make the mistake of thinking about institutions, such as business, and government, as ends in themselves. (Adali Stevenson)

•

We are all born with infinite potential and creativity. We all have it in us. Each and every one of us. That is the only truth. (Deepak Chopra)

•

We are made of all those who have built and broken us. (Atticus)

•

We cannot change the cards we are dealt, just how we play the hand. (Randy Pausch)

•

We cannot choose our external circumstances, but we can always choose how we respond to them. (Epictetus)

•

We delight in the beauty of the butterfly, but rarely admit the changes it has gone through to achieve that beauty. (Maya Angelou)

•

We either make ourselves miserable, or we make ourselves strong. The amount of work is the same. (Carlos Castaneda)

•

We find comfort among those who agree with us-growth among those who don't. (Frank A. Clark)

•

We generally change ourselves for one of two reasons: inspiration or desperation. (Jim Rohn)

•

We have no more right to consume happiness without producing it than to consume wealth without producing it. (GB Shaw)

•

We hope vaguely, but dread precisely. (Paul Valery)

•

We learn from experience. A man never wakes up his second baby just to see it smile. (Grace Williams)

•

We make time for the things we love, and excuses for the things we don't. (Mark Anthony)

•

We may encounter many defeats but we must not be defeated. (Maya Angelou)

•

We must all suffer one of two things: the pain of discipline or the pain of regret or disappointment. (Jim Rohn)

•

We must be willing to get rid of the life we have planned, so as to have the life that is waiting for us. (Joesph Campbell)

•

We need to accept that we won't always make the right decisions, that we will screw up royally sometimes- understanding that failure is not the opposite of success, it is part of success. (Arianna Huffington)

•

We suffer more often in imagination than in reality. (Seneca)

•

We witness other people's storms from the shelter of our own perspectives. Let's be mindful that we don't add the cold rain of judgement to their already soaked spirits. (Liz Newman)

•

Wealth flows from energy and ideas. (William Feather)

•

Wealth is the ability to fully experience life. (HD
Thoreau)

•

What am I living for and what am I dying for are the
same question. (Margaret Atwood)

•

What gets measured gets improved. (Peter Drucker)

•

What is uttered from the heart alone will win the
hearts of others to your own. (Goethe)

•

What man actually needs is not a tensionless state
but rather the striving and struggling for some goal
worthy of him. (Victor Frankl)

•

What worries you, masters you. (john Locke)

•

What you get by achieving your goals is not as
important as what you become by achieving your
goals. (Zig Ziglar)

•

Whatever you do, never run back to what broke you.
(Frank Ocean)

•

Whatever you do, or dream you can, begin it.
Boldness has genius and power and magic in it.
(Goethe)

•

When a man is wrapped up in himself he makes a
pretty small package. (John Ruskin)

•

When a person tells you,"I will think it over and let
you know" – you know. (Olin Miller)

•

When Alexander the Great visited Diogenes and
asked whether he could do anything for the famed
teacher, Diogenes replied, 'Only stand out of my
light.' Perhaps someday we shall know how to
heighten creativity. Until then, one of the best
things we can do for creative men and women is to
stand out of their light. (JW Gardner)

•

When eating fruit, think of the person who planted
the tree. (Vietnamese proverb)

•

When I look back on whatever my past has been
and the successes, my greatest rewards have been
the people and the relationships that I have had, the
money has been an accident. (Ray Dalio)

•

When the wind rises some people build walls.
Others build windmills. (Chinese proverb)

•

When we slow down, we are reminded of what matters most.(Julianna Poplin)

•

When you have confidence, you can have a lot of fun. And when you have fun, you can do amazing things. (Joe Namath)

•

When you read a classic, you do not see more in the book than you did before, you see more in you than there was before. (Clifton Fadiman)

•

When you remember something about somebody, you are demonstrating to them that you care. (Joshua Foer)

•

When you want something, all the universe conspires in helping you to achieve it. (Paulo Coelho)

•

When you win, say nothing. When you lose, say less. (Paul Brown)

•

When your work speaks for itself, don't interrupt. (Henry J. Kaiser)

•

Where it is in our power to act, it is also in our power to not act. (Aristotle)

•

Wherever you stand, be the soul of that place. (Rumi)

•

Which form of proverb do you prefer, better late than never, or better never than late? (Lewis Carroll)

•

Who has once the fame to be an early riser may sleep till noon. (James Howell)

•

Words are plentiful, deeds are precious. (Lech Walsena)

•

You are never too old to set another goal or to dream a new dream. (CS Lewis)

•

You are not lazy, unmotivated, or stuck. After years of living your life in survival mode, you are exhausted. There is a difference. (Nakeia Homer)

•

You are not the darkness you endured. You are the light that refused to surrender. (John Mark Green)

•

You are only given a little spark of madness. You must not lose it. (Robin Williams)

•

You are responsible for how long you let what hurt you, haunt you. (Audi L Brown)

•

You are the average of the five people you spend the most time with. (Jim Rohn)

•

You are what you do, not what you say you will do. (Carl Jung)

•

You become what you give your attention to. (Epictetus)

•

You become what you think about all day long. (RW Emerson)

•

You build on failure. You use it as a stepping stone. Close the door on the past. You don't try to forget the mistakes, but you don't dwell on it. You don't let it have any of your energy, or any of your time, or any of your space. (J Cash)

•

You can tell more about a person by what he says about others than you can by what others say about him. (Audrey Hepburn)

•

You can't afford to relax your guard once you are successful. (Andrew Grove)

•

You can't be trendsetters if all you do is follow the trend and choose from what is already available in the marketplace.(Robyn Waters)

•

You can't really decide to make a masterpiece. You just have to think hard, work hard, and try to make a painting that you care about. Then, if you are lucky, your work will find an audience for whom it is meaningful. (Susan Kare)

•

You cannot dream yourself into a character, you must hammer and forge yourself into one. (Henry D. Thoreau)

•

You can't depend on your eyes when your imagination is out of focus. (Mark Twain)

•

You don't get paid for the hour. You get paid for the value you bring to the hour. (Jim Rohn)

•

You don't have to be the best in the world at what you do but you have to be your personal best at what you do. (John Lee)

•

You don't inspire your teammates by showing them how amazing you are. You inspire them by showing them how amazing they are. (Robyn Benincasa)

•

You have got to learn to leave the table when love is no longer being served. (Nina Simone)

•

You know how they say we only use 10 percent of our brains? I think we only use 10 percent of our hearts. (Owen Wilson)

•

You may have a fresh start any moment you choose, for this thing that we call failure is not the falling down, but the staying down. (Mary Pickford)

•

You must never confuse faith that you will prevail in the end-which you can never afford to lose-with the discipline to confront the most brutal facts of your current reality, whatever they might be. (Admiral James B Stockdale)

•

You often feel tired, not because you have done too much, but because you have done too little of what sparks a light in you. (Alexander den Heijer)

•

You pray for the rain, you gotta deal with the mud too. That's a part of it. (Denzel Washington)

•

You told me once that we shall be judged by our intentions, not our accomplishments. I thought it a grand remark. But we must intend to accomplish- not sit intending on a chair. (EM Forster)

•

You will never be criticised by someone who is doing more than you. You will always be criticised by someone doing less. (Denzel Washington)

•

You will never change your life until you change something you do daily. The secret of your success is found in your daily routine.(John C. Maxwell)

•

Your assumptions are your windows on the world. Scrub them off every once in a while, or the light won't come in. (Isaac Asimov)

•

Your reputation is what others are not thinking about you. (Tom Masson)

Your Notes & Learnings